The Phoenix T

WINTERFOLD

Poets Published in
The Phoenix Living Poets Series

★

James Aitchison
Alexander Baird · Alan Bold
R. H. Bowden · Frederick Broadie
George Mackay Brown · Michael Burn
Philip Callow · Hayden Carruth
John Cotton · Jennifer Couroucli
Gloria Evans Davies
Patric Dickinson
Tom Earley · D. J. Enright
Irene Fekete
John Fuller · David Gill
Peter Gruffydd
J. C. Hall · Molly Holden
John Horder · P. J. Kavanagh
Richard Kell · Laurie Lee
Laurence Lerner
Christopher Levenson
Edward Lowbury · Norman MacCaig
Roy McFadden
Diana McLoghlen
James Merrill · Ruth Miller
Leslie Norris · Robert Pack
Rodney Pybus · Arnold Rattenbury
Adrienne Rich · Anne Sexton · Jon Silkin
Jon Stallworthy
Edward Storey · Terence Tiller
Sydney Tremayne
Jon Manchip White

WINTERFOLD

By

GEORGE MACKAY BROWN

CHATTO AND WINDUS

THE HOGARTH PRESS
1976

Published by
Chatto and Windus Ltd
with The Hogarth Press Ltd
40 William IV Street
London WC2N 4DF

*

Clarke, Irwin & Co. Ltd
Toronto

ISBN 0 7011 2147 5

Printed in Great Britain by
Lewis Reprints Ltd.
The Brown Knight and Truscott Group
London and Tonbridge

To
Kulgin and Colin

NOTE

I apologise for the appearance, yet again, of the lyric 'From Stone to Thorn'. It was the first 'Stations of the Cross' poem I wrote. It suggested others, and so the sequence would not be complete without it. It has been put to memorable music by Peter Maxwell Davies.

I suppose I ought to apologise also for altering some poems since their first appearance in anthology or magazine: sometimes by an invisible thread or two, sometimes by radical patchwork. An imperfect poem goes on seeking the silence.

The Earl Rognvald Kolson poems have their origin in the medieval *Orkneyinga Saga*. These 'imitations' may disturb Norse purists. What I have tried to do is preserve some of the gaiety, savagery, piety of the originals.

It should not be obligatory for poets to celebrate, as best they can, only the greyness of contemporary life. Some of the poems in this book are swatches cut from here and there in the one weave of time.

Most of the poems have appeared in periodicals and anthologies. Some of the Norse 'imitations' made a first tentative appearance in *An Orkney Tapestry* (Gollancz). Acknowledgements to the editors of *The House that Jack Built* (SHELTER anthology), *New Poems* (Hutchinson), *Scottish Poetry* 7 (Edinburgh University Press), *Twelve Poems* (Belfast University), *Ring of Words* (Oliver and Boyd), *Voices of Our Kind* (Saltire Society), *New Statesman, Spectator, Scotsman, Glasgow Herald, Lines Review, Antaeus, Gambit, Ariel, Scottish Field, POTH, Mid N A G Poster Poems, Akros.*

CONTENTS

WINTERFOLD

BETHLEHEM

Angel, Innkeeper, Our Lady,
Captain of Herod's Guard,
Shepherd, Magus

Gloria Gloria Gloria
FULL UP – Put that sign in the window
This is the first sorrow, that the dove should vanish
We will muster here with horse and trumpet
The last of the ewes is folded now
There it is, look, again, the scrieving star

The star, alpha to omega, spells on
Gloria in excelsis Deo
Supper the ox and the ass, I told you
The second sorrow, a crooked plough
I have an order from Herod, sealed
The sky is cold as psalms and angels tonight

Will we take our thirsts down to the alehouse?
Ill-used treasures of the old kingdoms
Et in terra pax hominibus bonae voluntatis
Not another hoof on the cobbles, surely!
The third sorrow, black seed
The despatch is marked "most secret, urgent"

You will therefore brighten your swords
A drop of mulled ale for winter bones
The ancient scrolls dust in the jars
Laudamus te, benedicimus te
Go down. Tell the stranger "No room"
The fourth sorrow, soldiers in a cornfield

The fifth sorrow, a starved child in a door
The security of the state is threatened
In the yard, look – a man, a loaded lass
How should we read the runes of a new kingdom?
Adoramus te, glorificamus te
What, Nazarenes? The woman exhausted?

Straw in the cowshed, that's all I can offer
The road of sorrows stops at The House of Bread
An upstart king. A rebellion plotted
We'll drink inside to a good lambing
Our road ends. The Word has been uttered
Gratias agimus tibi propter magnam gloriam tuam

Gloria Gloria Gloria
A lantern, quick. Something's happened
The last sorrow and the first joy are one
I think we know what to do with usurpers
A birth? In the byre? Whose bairn?
We give these rings and robes to a winter child

THE GOLDEN DOOR

1
I unlatched the jade door.
Worms were breeding silk,
A girl fingered a loom.
I entered the golden door
(There my throne stood, withering).
I passed through rooms
Of flowers, flagons, chessboards
And a room with a fountain.

At the top of the black spiral
A wise one said, 'Majesty,
Three nights now we have seen this planet.
The time is come
For exile, the tent in the desert.'

2
What wandered about the star streets
Last night, late?
It knocked for shelter at doors of gold, like a lost boy.
My heart was bruised with the image.
I am waiting now at sunset, again, with my charts.
I had perhaps drunk too much midnight wine.

3
When the lawmen have gone
Before the girl enters
With water and a lamp
I sit at the window.
The stars come, each after other.
'I am the Bringer of Dew.'
'I am the Dove.'
'I am the Swarm of Bees.'
'I am the Grain of Dust from the Floor of Heaven.'
'I am the Emerald.'
'I am the Temple Lamp.'
I greet those faithful
Who troop to my dark window.
What should I say
To this one, intruder and stranger?
He has stood there two nights
And is silent still.
I imagine a title,
'Keeper of the Door of Corn'.
And a word, 'Come'.

YULE

Castle to forest, more wind, and the roads drifted.
We followed the map as best we could.
We came at noon to the marked tree,
A grey gnarled column.
The sergeant shouted. Our axes flashed. They bit.
We struck out pieces of bark and bole.
We laboured like men in a siege, among whirls of snow,
But root was one with berry still
In the first red seepings of sunset.
                    In the village windows, that twilight,
Tinsel stars glittered.
There were chains of coloured tissue and paper lanterns.
Under the street lamp, chaste mouths.
Then the village slept, unblessed by the winter tree.
The sky was a hushed river of light.
Flagons gleamed in firelight at the inn.
Three strangers came, burdened. They were taken inside.
'No word of this at the castle,' said Blok at midnight.
'Some childishness, star and snowman and crib,
Crippled our arms today.
In March we'll be back. The peasants will have their tree.'

THE KEEPER OF THE MIDNIGHT GATE

What are all the hillmen wanting
Around the alehouse door,
The old one carrying a new lamb?
Drink, likely, and women.
Too cold for them up on the hill
With stars snapping their silver fingers.
They've left a boy
To keep the door of the fold, I hope.

What are you? Come closer, maskers.
Melchior. Caspar. Balthazzar.
No names like that hereabout.
O thank you, sir!
Pass on, Daffodil-face, Ebony-face, Nut-face.
Go in peace
With your foreign stinks and the one clang in your sack.

No bite or blanket in that inn, Lady
Unless you're loaded.
Pass on, man. There might be a corner. I know she's done in.
His furnace mouth
Keeps the ox warm.
The publican's fire is the bleeze of gold in his till.

Yes, colonel, the following village women
As far as I know
Have been brought to bed this past week
Or are ripe to the bursting
Or may be in their sweet pains tonight –
Rachel, Tamar, Deborah,
Ruth, Esther,
Sara, Jemima, Judith.
Yes, sir –

This gate is open always for King Herod's heroic
Hooves and swords.

An angel, are you?
Mister, let me tell you
The magistrates
Want no comic-singers in this town this winter.
What are the shadows
There, at the fire's edge, with guitars?
I did not think
Angels stank and had holes in their sleeves.
All right, go through, vagrants.
Say, if you're challenged
You came in by another road.

Worms are feasting
Round the fire at the heart of the earth tonight,
Redbreast.
You can have this crumb from my sandwich.
This cold night
You'd be better in the silver cage of a merchant.

A POEM FOR SHELTER

Who was so rich
He owned diamonds and snowflakes and fire,
The leaf and the forest,
Herring and whale and horizon –
Who had the key to the chamber beyond the stars
And the key of the grave –
Who was sower and seed and bread
Came on a black night
To a poor hovel with a star peeking through rafters
And slept among beasts
And put a sweet cold look on kings and shepherds.

But the children of time, their rooftrees should be strong.

TEA POEMS

Chinaman

Water, first creature of the gods.
It dances in many masks.

> For a young child, milk.
> For the peasant, honey and mud.
> For lovers and poets, wine.
> For the man on his way to the block, many well-directed spits.
> For an enemy, mixings of blood.
> For the Dragon-god, ichor.
> For a dead friend, a measure of eye-salt.

A courteous man is entertaining strangers
Among his goldfish and willows.
The musician sits in the pavilion door
(His flute is swathed in silk.)
An urn is brought to the table by girls.
This is the water of offered friendship.
Notice the agreeable angle of pouring,
The pure ascending columns of vapour,
The precise arrangement of finger and bowl and lip.
Birds make all about those sippers and smilers ceremonies of very sweet sound.

Smugglers

Midnight. Measured musical cold sea circles.
The yawl struck suddenly!
Oars wrapped the boat in a tangled web.
The boy cried out – Smith gagged him with tarry fingers.
It was no rock, not the fearful face of Hoy.
The boat spun back from pliant timbers.
A maze of voices above us then.
Our skipper growled, 'Where's your light?'
(A lantern was to hang in the cross-trees
For half-an-hour after midnight.
In "The Arctic Whaler" that had been harped on well.)
'You comm too litt,' a Dutchman said,
The words like a fankle of rusted wire.
'Now we're here,' said Smith
'And it's only twenty-past-twelve, lower down
Twelve kegs rum, tobacco as much as you've got,
A poke of snuff for the laird. Have you rolls of silk?'
He drew out silver, rang it in his fist like a bell.
Now we could see green-black curves of hull
And cropped heads hung over the side,
Even the mouth that was torturing the language.
'Fif box tea, bess China.'
With fearful patience our skipper told on his fingers
The smuggler's litany:
Silk, rum, tobacco. The florins chimed in his fist.
'Rum. Tobacco. Silk. That was the understanding.'
Smith swore to God not he nor any Orkneyman
Would risk rope or irons for women's swill.
He pleaded. He praised. He threatened.
Again the stony voice from the star-web above. 'Tea.
Noding but China tea. For silver. Fif box.'

Afternoon Tea

Drank Mrs Leask, sticking out her pinkie.
Drank Mrs Spence, having poured in a tinkle-tinkle of
whisky (I've such a bad cold!)
Drank Mrs Halcrow, kissing her cup like a lover.
Drank Mrs Traill, and her Pekinese filthied the floor
with bits of biscuit and chocolate.
Drank Mrs Clouston, through rocky jaws.
Drank Mrs Heddle, her mouth dodging a sliver of lemon.
Drank Bella the tea wife, who then read engagements,
letters, trips and love in
every circling clay hollow.

APRIL THE SIXTEENTH

What did they bring to the saint?
The shepherds a fleece.
That winter many lambs were born in the snow.

What did the dark ones bring?
To Magnus the tinkers have brought
A new bright can. Their hammers beat all night.

What have they brought to the saint?
A fishless fisherman
Spread his torn net at the wall of the church.

And the farm boys offered
A sweetness, gaiety, chasteness
Of hymning mouths.

The women came to their martyr
With woven things
And salt butter for the poor of the island.

And the poor of the island
Came with their hungers,
Then went hovelwards with crossed hands over the hill.

FIDDLERS AT THE HARVEST HOME

Quarry

Hewings in the groin of the earth
A stone for a threshold
A stone for a hearth
A stone for a chisel to flash at in the kirkyard
A stone to sharpen a scythe
Two heavy rounds for the mill
A niche for butter and fish, to keep them cold

Corn

The green and the yellow upstarts
A wind dancer
Keeper of the secrets of dust and sun and seed
Spume at the scarecrow's thigh
The oat for the oven
Malt for the kirn
A crust kirk-broken
A brightness across the jaw of the winter mouse

Sheep

Drifters across a hill and seashore
A smouldering ram
Tilt of sharn-and-fog for the shearer
The horn at the crag
The scripture fleece
The ewe among red tatters of snow
The daffodils' friend (the lamb)
Giver of coats to the cold ones at the shore

Fish

Silent seekers through wave and wrack
    A cod for the kirk
    A cod for the laird
    A cod for the boat
    One for three green plates in a croft
    One for peatsmoke
    A head for a wind-blue hand at the door
    And bones for needles, livers for a winter lamp

Dance

Islanders come to their stillness
    From the dance of plough and flail
    And the fling of the net
    And waverings round the lamp and barrel
    And the fire-dance on the hill
    And sheer stone sea-egg seeking
    And the midnight reel of seed and soul
    At last near the kirk
    The music is cut on stone ramshackle pages

Wheels

Wheels that hallow ghost and bone –
    From turning wood, a skein
    From thunder of stones, meal
    From the reeling kirn, butter and cheese
    From lessening oil rings, a winter flame
    From creel-broken circles, the lobster
    At midnight, the tryst of seed with soul
    The sun-wheel turns
    Stone to dust to corn to bread to breath

TWELFTH CENTURY NORSE LYRICS
of Rognvald Kolson, Earl and Saint

1

The Accomplishments of an Earl

Chessboard, tiltyard, trout-stream
Know my sweet passes.
Old writings are no mystery to me
Nor any modern book.
Ski across winterfold flashes.
Deep curves I make with arrow and oar.
I know the twelve notes of a harp.
At the red forge
My clamorous shadow is sometimes rooted.

2

Merchant Ship

Five weeks our keel lay choked
In Grimsby mudflats.
Lugworm and silt, a foul grey honey.
Unfurl, white sail
Eastwards, over the loose waves,
A questing skua
To the hard rock of Bergen.

3

The Westray Monks

Sixteen walkers about the church,
Heads bare as stone,
Long striders, deep-voiced, rough-handed.
'Brother wind, gentle sister raindrops' –
That's what they call this black whirl of storm.
They haven't a sword between them.
Here they come, in procession,
Demure and harmless as girls.

4

A Shipwreck in Shetland

Help and *Arrow*, those slender seekers,
Scatter to a hundred boards.
Women may weep for that
But the poets
Are glad of shipwrecks many a winter night.
The sailors, shamed,
Will ravel their sea-skills with a tougher thread.

I've swallowed mouthfuls of sea.
They gladdened me more
Than the best wine or mead.
The sea sings like a girl over my half-drowned feet.
With shivering mouth
I draw the hammered snake-ring from my finger.
I pledge myself to Our Lady of the Waves.

In a princely coat, stiff with runes and dragons,
I leapt from the wreck.
Cold now, sea-insulted,
I shiver at a Shetland fire.
With tattered sealskin
The women cancel my nakedness.

Einar, laird, though at your board
You give room to no stranger
Unless the chief stranger come, the Earl,
Yet set out horns
And ring your hearth with benches.
Tonight I am riding
To visit your unpopular house.

5

Love Songs to the Lady Ermengarde of Narbonne

Your hair, lady
Is long, a bright waterfall.
You move through the warriors
Rich and tall as starlight.
What can I give
For the cup and kisses brought to my mouth?
Nothing.
This red hand, a death-dealer.

The summer mouth of Ermengarde
Commands two things –
A sea of saga-stuff, wreckage, gold,
As far as Jordan,
And later, at leaf-fall,
On patched homing wings
A sun-dark hero.

White as snow
White as silver
The lady,
A beauty all whiteness,
A kindness
Red as wine.
Another redness, fire
About the castle,
A sharp whiteness, swords.

6

In praise of Audun, the first warrior to board the African ship

Audun the Red
Was the earliest reaper

In this harvest.
Black sheaves
Fell on the dromond.
Flame-bearded Audun
Was complete gules.
Erling's Audun
Through fire and blood
Bound his red harvest.

7

Jerusalem

We stand here, shriven,
A hundred warmen lustred with penance,
In each hand
Assoiled from murders, bordels, thievings now
A leaf of palm.
Footsteps, free and fated, turn
To the fourteen redemptive lingerings
And the hill marked † with this sign.

8

A Mass at Sea

We left our shares to rust
On a northern hill,
Exchanged oxen for green and blue tramplers!
Poet, peasant, priest,
One ark of pilgrims
Out of the dragon sea, a seeking
Into the lucencies of Christ.
(Salt furrows we make
Under your headlands, Byzantium.)
Sin darkens the grain-hold.
We have branded their coasts with rage and lust,
The old dragon-breath.
No end of sorrow, soultroth, seeking, still.
Kyrie, Christe, Kyrie eleison
The Golden Harvester
Comes out to grace, with robe and ring, the swineherd.

THE DESERTION OF THE WOMEN AND SEALS

Howie gave sentence of slaughter
To the fifty seals on the skerry.
For a month now the inland lasses,
Bella, Jemima, Mary
And Hundaskaill's cold beautiful daughter
– It was said, because of his hard grudging fist –
Denied their kisses.
A month he watched the drift of seals in the west.

A clean gale out of the sunset
Would cancel scent and sound
But make those creatures vivid upon the floods.
'Maybe,' thought Howie, 'a pound
Or thirty shillings, for powder and shot' . . . .
He would change the flock to bag and slipper and brooch –
Entrancing gauds –
And gather the spendthrift girls back to his couch.

That sunset, shrug after shrug,
The seals abandoned the shore.
Across the sacrificial rock
Drifted a delicate smirr,
Tresses of haar, a fleece of fog.
It scarfed in one cold weave the selkie-flight.
Then, rook by rook,
Round Howie's impotence drew in the night.

VIKINGS : Three harp-songs

Bjorn the Shetlander Sails to Largs 1263

I am a farmer from Yell in Shetland.
Bjorn my mother called me.
I grew among seals and clouds and birds and women.
The men came home in the ships for harvest
With wounds on them and bits of silver.
One year my father did not come home.
The sea has him, off Lindisfarne.
I learned drinking and love that winter.
I can handle horse or boat,
Useful crafts for a man to know,
And am thought to be a good chess-player
And passable on the harp.
Next year, if I live that long
My beard will have a fine golden curl to it.
Perhaps Thora will love me then.
I have never been further south than Whalsay.
Is it true, what the vikings say –
Wine-skins, brothels, black faces south of Spain
And kirks colder than sea-caves?
This is good, to have seen fifteen summers.
Tomorrow with Paul and Sverr my brothers
I sail for Scotland.
A thousand sea-borne swords, a golden mask.

The New Skipper

Arn, Thorvald, Sven, Paul, Grettir, Harald
The *Sea Wolf* is out of the shed, new tar on her hull.
The rollers are under the keel.
The women have put ale, salt meat, and bread on board.
As soon as the wave runs clean from Birsay
We will leave the Orkneys behind us,
The scarred hills and the creeled sounds,
And tonight we will anchor at the mouth of a Scottish river.
Our voyage lies east this year.
We have heard of such towns – Aberdeen, Grimsby, London,
And the merchants who live in tall houses.
The churches have had enough of our swords
And the girls who weave their words into curse or spell.
Our voyage does not lie west this spring
Among holiness and drifts of rain.
There are few chalices left in those islands.
It is time the merchants knew about us.
We will be back in time for the corn harvest.
You women, see that the scythes are sharp and the barns swept,
And the ale thick with honey.
We are tired of broken coast-lines.
This summer we deal in wool and useful currency.
They are not too beautiful, the girls in the east.

A Battle in Ulster

Remarking, 'It is not to my taste
To wheeze on a white pillow
Nor to toil gravewards on a stick, murdered slowly
By avarice, envy, lust,'
Einar ran where the swords fell thickest.

An Irish axe
Struck the right shoulder of Sweyn the skald.
'In future,' said Sweyn,
'I will write my poems with the left hand.
I will sup a sinister broth.'

Near the end of the battle
Rolf returned to the ship, downcast.
'Gudrun,' he said, 'is a proud woman.
She will not bed with boys.
Hard wounds I sought
For thigh and chest and forehead today.
All I have got
Is a broken tooth, an eye blue as an oyster,
And my pinkie scratched.
From now on, Gudrun,
I will court less particular girls.'

THE ESCAPE OF THE HART
(for S.C.)

Suddenly, on the hill, pursuit and flight!
Taut bows, a hound across the dawn, the stag's
Enormous leap to pacify the arrow.
Love,
Let the white beast move in power this evening across the
hunter's hill, breaking through
All tangled desires, dancing wounds, to a secret water.

Cold it was in the corrie that morning,
A harsh rain. We drew the prince
Round by the eyrie, the thunders of new water.
The Saxons lay in the next glen.
We signed our bread with holy crosses. Then,
Red on the moor, through shrouds and prisms of fog, we saw
the hunters
Issue like beads of blood.
God keep our prince, our beautiful stag, from such danger
again!
He looked at them with a cold eye.
Then rain let down its silver enchanted walls.

THE SEA : Four Elegies

THE SEA

The word "sea" is small and easily uttered.
They utter it lightly who know least about it.
A vast ancient terror is locked in the name
Like energy in an atom.
Sailors, explorers, fishermen know this.
Women who stand on headlands, they know it.
The maritime tribes knew it well.
Their artists strove at harp and loom
To cover the terror with beautiful names.
The sea is the Great Sweet Mother.
She is the Swan's Path.
She is the Whale's Acre.
She is the Garden of White Roses.
She is the Keeper of Horses.
(The Loom also, the Harp with a thousand voices.)
She is the Giver of Salt and Pearls.
The Vikings, her closest children, hated the sea.
She summoned them, twice a year, from plough and lovebed.
They called her, with cold mouths, the Widow Maker.

THE DOOR OF WATER

Think of death, how it has many doors.
A child enters the Dove Door
And leaves a small wonderment behind him.
For soldiers and airmen there is the Door of Fire.
Most of us, with inadequate heart or lung or artery
Disappear through the simple Door of the Skull.
There is the Door of the Sheaf: the granary is beyond.
The very old enter, stooping,
Harvesters under a load of tranquil sorrows.
For islanders, the Door of Water.
Beyond a lintel carved with beautiful names
The sea yields to the bone, at last, a meaning.

THE LOST

One stumbled on a grey hill, very steep.
One drank deeply, and found himself at a carousel of angels.
One whispered in the secretest cell of salt.
One (young) exchanged many untasted Aprils for a brief
ecstasy.
One who had turned hundreds from the door of The Salt
Mother knocked on her window that night, alone.
One wrote "amen" on a spindrift page.
Were they offered for all seareft – piracy, pain of fish, the
black and gold cargoes?
A storm-ripened one went swiftly that March among
Sea-scythes, flails, winnowings.
After the third wave, the sea-querns had him.
The Atlantic was veined all summer with slow pure glitters.

A DROWNING

I am the unborn who go my ways at
once to the dark door: to drowning,
rot, fire, the choked heart, the
choked brain, the choked bowel, the
stroke of God: but one door is ajar
always for the people who live in
islands.
I am the child among sand and rockpools.
I am the boy who lays two lobsters on
a poor threshold.
I am the young man who comes out of the
storm, a ghost with a red mouth.
I am the father whose sperm tastes of
the sea.
Should an old man weary the people at
last with legends of shipwreck?
The waters opened last night. I
entered. The grey door shut
behind me.

UNPOPULAR FISHERMAN

They've carried a seven-foot coffin
Down to the shore.
In Quoylay, look for no net-reft
Or rapes any more.

(Who is it dead? A man
With a shortage of friends.
God send us more grief when we
Come to our ends.

Is it the laird? That great one
With five or six fawners
Might reach his long porphyry home
– But who'd be the mourners?

Is it Ezra the tinker? Not him.
There'll be pipers to blow,
Fist-fights and reels and whisky
The day he's laid low.

Is it Swart who gives the short measure
For the ale and the rum?
That one could stretch the length of his counter, unmourned
Till kingdom come.

What unpopular man is dead?
The slow feet pass
Among the tombs. . . . *As for a man, his days*
Are brief as grass.)

The cold tumultuous hands they fold
In the lee of the kirk
For seven winters were at the plundering westwards
Of herring and shark.

Look for no lawless cradles in Quoylay more.
Wholesome the fights
With no more gouging, blasphemy, broken bottles
On Saturday nights.

EYNHALLOW : CROFTER AND MONASTERY

I rent and till a patch of dirt
Not much bigger than my coat.
I keep a cow and twelve swine
And some sheep and a boat.
Drudgings, stone

The name of my wife is Hild.
Hild has a bitter tongue.
She makes passable butter and ale.
Her mouth brims and brims with bairnsong.
Driftings, stone

What's winter? A thousand stars,
Shrinkings of snow, an empty pail.
All summer I go, a drenched ox
Between the plough and the flail.
Drudgings, stone

I say a prayer when I remember.
When the bishop comes to bless his flock
I tell my sins and give him a fish.
Once I saw a sealwoman on a rock.
Driftings, stone

Twelve bald heads have come to this island.
They divide the day with Terce and Laud.
Herring are "the little silver brothers".
Like dust-of-gold they sift each clod.
Dancings, stone

DEOR
(from the Old English)

Weland that famous swordsmith
Endured the gull and the wave.
He blew his fists in winter,
He looked for a foreign grave.
He trudged about the headlands,
A cripple and a slave.
That sorrow withered, so may this

Beadohild wept when death
Cold on her brothers was snowing.
And sorrow grew. No gown
Could hide from public showing
The glebe of her body rich
From Weland's reckless sowing.
That sorrow withered, so may this

The stranger paused. He marvelled
At a heart-rooted pain.
The thorn ran deep, the bud
Spread a crimson stain.
He would not pluck it, for fear
The rose scattered like rain.
That sorrow withered, so may this

Earmonric the tyrant
Sat like a wolf by the wall.
Secret mouths round the board
Drank to the beast's fall.
He licked long lazy chops.
The ale grew bitter as gall.
That sorrow withered, so may this

Deor the poet's my name.
I enchanted the leaves of June
Till Heorrend Honeythroat came
And warbled me out of tune,
And sang my fields away,
And shaped a purer rune.
All sorrows wither, so may this

SEVEN TRANSLATIONS OF A LOST POEM

1

At the door marked with the sign Bordel
I was expensively entertained.
For that rich hour I hobble on a stick.

At the door marked Poet
I never sat with such a dull spiteful creature.
Yet harp can cancel crippledom.

When I come to the door marked Death
It will be sorrow to me
I had not been carried through it, a small
white wordless statue.

2

She was a very luxurious lady.
She rotted my leg.

This man made street-stones jade and diamond.
I did not like him.

An old ploughman, that's what I'd like to be,
near my death,
Ignorant of ode and perfume.

3

I still get angry at the loss of five gold pieces
And my boyhood
And my ability to dance, to that madam.

'I am poor. Nobody understands genius.
What are you wanting here?'
After the stings and blunderings, honey.

Death is a stroke of fire
Or a slow withering.
Some say, a circling magnificence like the ocean.

4

'I charge more than most
Because my love
Will make you a lord or a beggar.'
That's what the witch said
And I naked among the webs of silk.

'One poem, price one silver denarius.
Then off with you.
My shirt is torn. Look. I must see to it.'
That's what the enchanter said
One morning, among privy noises.

Death, lord, my inheritance is squandered
Among courtesans and artists.
Never a thought I gave to you
Until now, when I stand at your door
Without greeting or a proper gift.

5

The address given was Peacock House.
I came to Full Moon House.
Each girl had an ivory box, for gifts.
In one room a silver mirror.
Toothlessness, scant hairs, peered back at me.

Also by mistake I called on the wrong poet
For instruction in verse-craft.
The man could explain nothing.
He took the fee. He sent me home early.
He is said to be the best poet in all that long street.

I hope, when I am summoned by death
That – sick and one-legged as I am –
Once more I will be directed to the wrong door.

6

If Sandra would open her blue robe,
Nothing more. There is nothing
I would ask or desire from the gods.

If Sator would recite The Hill Song
I would seek, a ghost,
That same day, the marble.

She showed the silk under the silk.
He uttered "plough-to-oven", a spell.
Why have I lived another half-century?

7

With a golden key I opened a door
On a bowl of dead rose-leaves.

In a house of withered webbed stone
The harp is hidden.

Be patient now, near the end –
Fold hands.
Bid the stone enter.
                    Love and Beauty,
One old April, cut epitaphs.

SEA WIDOW

1

Silence

Did I plead with you to keep from that rock
Where the *Merle* lost strake and mast?
I have dreamed of the white bone under a wheeling flock.
I said, 'On that skerry he'll be cast
This fog or that gale –
A kind story will be over at last.
It is not good for a man to plunder the horizons and bounds of the whale.'

But I said nothing. Love ebbed and flowed. We kept the feast and the fast.

Last night my father came with the funeral ale.

2

Lost Lovers

What if I had turned to greet the tall stranger
With kindness on his face, on the road?
There was one mouth that trembled with desire and danger.
Another suggested a clover ditch for the drift of his seed.
A merchant promised whiteness, a ring, a proper blessing in the precincts of God.

That man was grey and gentle and rich.

I was carried to a door marked with salt, and with tar and weed.

3

What the Fisherman Said

There is no bread like the crust and fragrance
From your hands.

A fisherman dreads a witchlook
On the road to his boat.
Stand well behind me, girl, and always.

Leave that old man
And three thankless brothers.
There are women whose love at last is all for cats.

Spin out of me
Into yourself, the stuff of life, secretly.
Weave it on a sweet loom.

I have not relished ale-house talk
Nor my pipe
With its flame-flowers and smoke and spit,
Nor even Sigurd's fiddle
Since the first kiss among seaweed.
Next morning I woke richer than laird or merchant.

There is nothing to the snow and daffodils and larkrise of you.

Sealed with the brightness of your mouth
How will it be for me now
In the dangerous house of the sea-girls?

Why was this study not ardently taught
Among the globes and inkpots?
Love is better than numbers, seaports, battles.

I will build you a house with my hands,
A stored cupboard,
Undying hearth-flames, a door open to friend and stranger.

I wished once I had not met you.
Sea generations are too long.
It is a net I have folded in your womb.

From strange earth and stones,
A kirkyard on another shore with different names
You came through wind and cornstalks
For the mixing of dust,
For two names to be carved on one stone.
I did not think then
You might lie under it lonely
And I shells, salt, seaweed.

I have put a black streak of tar
Through the ignorant name on the hull
And painted yours there, in red.
Old men, going past, look wicked and young.

4

Wedding Ring

Gold to enclose two lives for ever. There were maybe four
Good rounds, perfect returnings, in that one year,
Four circles of grace.
The rest were pub-stoked lurchings, blood on his face,
Back to my healing or raging hand –
A trudging up from the beach with broken gear,
Or from the merchant's with meagre silver
For his baskets of shifting bronze.
He was lost three days, at the fair, with tinker and miller.
And once
I left him, stone-eared to all his implorings,
His vowing and swearing,
And stayed a month at my father's place.
Four precious restorings
Made all those tatters of time the bridal coat
And sweeter with every wearing.
He left all, house and woman and boat
For a wave that trundled him on past time and space.
The bed, where each day's devious circle closed, is seedless and lonely.
They unweave him, mackerel and gull.
I know the man only
In flecks of salt and grains of sand,
And when through the drifting pools of a child's face
Looks back the skull.

STATIONS OF THE CROSS

FROM STONE TO THORN

Condemnation
The winter jar of honey and grain
Is a Lenten urn.

Cross
Lord, it is time. Take our yoke
And sunwards turn.

First Fall
To drudge in furrows till you drop
Is to be born

Mother of God
Out of the mild mothering hill
And the chaste burn.

Simon
God-begun, the barley rack
By man is borne.

Veronica
Foldings of women. Your harrow sweat
Darkens her yarn.

Second Fall
Sower-and-Seed, one flesh, you fling
From stone to thorn.

Women of Jerusalem
You are bound for the Kingdom of Death. The enfolded
Women mourn.

Third Fall
Scythes are sharpened to bring you down,
King Barleycorn.

The Stripping
Flails creak. Golden coat
From kernel is torn.

Crucifixion
The fruitful stones thunder around,
Quern on quern.

Death
The last black hunger rages through you
With hoof and horn.

Pietà
Mother, fold him from those furrows,
Your broken bairn.

Sepulchre
Shepherd, angel, king are kneeling, look,
In the door of the barn.

PILATE

Cool water over my fingers flowing
*
The upstart
Had ruined a night and a morning for me.
I thrust that stone face from my door.
*
I was told later he bent a knee
Between the cupid and the rosebush.
The gardener told me that later, laughing.
*
And that a woman hung upon him like a fountain.
*

What is it to me, who helps this king
Or strikes him down?
I reduced majesty to a driven shadow.
*
Another woman stood between him and the sun,
A tree, sifting light and shadow across his face.
*
Outside the tavern
It was down with him once more,
Four holes in the dust.
*
More women then, a gale of them,
His face like a scald
And they moving about him, a tumult of shadows and
breezes.
*
He clung close to the curve of the world.
*
The king had gone out in a purple coat.
Now the king
Wore only rags of flesh about the bone.
*
(I examined cornstalks in the store at Tarsus
And discovered a black kernel.
*
Of the seven vats shipped from Rhodes
Two had leaked in the hold,
One fell from the sling and was broken.)
*
And tell this Arimathean
He can do what he likes with the less-than-shadow.
*
No more today. That business is over. Pass the seal.

Rood

The lesser mysteries rooted also
in that first garden,
apple-fraught, with pure rinsings.

Harp

He at a stone, head upon strings,
summoning
to a sweet circle the seven red beasts.

Lamp

Last seed of the sun, hoarded
for sunlessness, ice,
beastbreathing cave of winter.

Image

A prince lost
in a maze of corrupt mirrors
and Fold of Light, unmoving.

Ballad

Reveller at the door – grey mouth
uttering ocean spells,
sea-skull on brideboard set.

Mask

Among flutes and statues
a vestal unwinds
scarlet web from skull.

Dance

Golden mask into grave –
twice now, dandled, thistledown's
frail dust drag.

Symbol

It outlasts roses,
statues,
even the grief of women.

Legend

Listen, in a mud-kissing mouth
the six-day story –
star, tree, fish, bird, beast.

Loom

Into the seamless coat-of-songs,
through sereness, starkness,
the shuttle drifts.

Jar

Midnight, and the last red circle breached.
A jar, upset
in first seepings of light.

Rune

Obliterator
of a thousand questing mouths,
and sevenfold silence still.

Talent

The minted circle, gift
of the lavish god
withered soon, and the hand a bone.

Stone

Are not long loved,
remembered, even decipherable,
your purest deepest cuttings.

HAWK

Flung from the fowler's fist
Ride now, lonely hawk

Through the hungers of the morning sky.
Shoulder the sun now. Take

Light about you, aloof and silent, now swivel,
Stumble on a step of air, trek

Into the heart of a cloud – folded awhile – then out
Like ore from a cleft, flaming, break!

(The fowler leans on a stile,
Foot-bound, face-bright,
And lets out, on swirling air-streams, lure and hook.)

The sky repeats your curves of talon and beak.

Halt now. Hover. Let your golden eye
Flame on that tussock below, a single stalk,

A windless twitch. Descend. Query. Then in a scythe swing
Scatter the delvers and spinners. Reach down. Lock

One guttering life in your claw. Engorge,
Engut, all but a flake

Of feather and slivers of bone. Be crested then among
        creatures,
Lord of the fast, the sacrifice, the wake!

(The fowler's spell
Will drift into you soon, a sweet ache,

A delight and a doom, a summons
To a bleak black

Rafter in a barn, almost forgotten then
Under that yearned-for yoke

Your brief lordship of cloud and rock.)

POTTER and JAR

Those humps and hollows are jars too, stranger.
    This is for Jude, the fig-merchant.
    Bespoke, this cluster of white curves.

'Jude requires a jar for his new arbour.'
    But hump-and-hollow surely, never
    A "fountain for thirst of angels" . . . .

What was brutish mud in a pit, last thaw,
    Rose, slow and lissom,
    Into the wheel of the sun.

Never before such coldness from my kiln.
    It is dust in the sign of oblation.

Today the removal from workshop to villa.
    Some yokel will bear it
    On mule-back, among fig spittings.

Any unlustered hand might sully it.
    The palm of a girl, poised delicately
    For love, mothering, death. I think, even that.

What questing ghost between dewfall and dawn
    Came, summoned, to the threshold of clay?

(Here they troop now, the village trollops,
All clattering, to the well,
Thick clay shouldering thick clay.
They linger always, silent, about the miracle.)

Do not speak about fall, or flaw, or the flow of time.
The drift and cling of a butterfly
Might start a fissure.

It should endure in a secret niche in the temple
Its fragile centuries.

Foreign hooves will whirl about it, some April.
It will be five shards on a hill.
And the ghost exiled from the circle of its peace.

The dream, the wheel, the dancing mud, the kiln.
It issued from these, an amphora.
My hands beat, obedient
To the harpings of planet and atom.
Bide then, angel of the jar, beyond all breakings.

Tilt it. This jar will be dealing widom and beauty still
When the last Caesar is urned.

No. The vulgar wealth that commissioned the work
Will reserve it for dust of roses.
It will stand on a sunless shelf.
'Adam made this, in the Street of Potters, one winter.
It did not stand well among our silks and silver.
Here, in the cellar,
It keeps cold the wine for wake and wedding.'

THE STONE CROSS

At dawn Havard sighted a hill in Ulster.
'A point to west,' said the helmsman. 'There the hive is.
There is the barren kingdom of drones.'

We sailed past cave and cormorant and curragh.
We anchored under a stone cross at noon.

Creatures came down to meet us
With stony heads, voices like insects, raised hands.

They murmured 'Mother', 'Sancta Maria', 'Our Lady'
But that hostess was not to be seen.

Brother Simon drew me from sea to rock.
He made a cross of grey air between us.

It was a household of men only.
A boy offered to wipe salt from our foreheads.

'Havard, it is time to make a start now.'
Havard flashed his axe in the face of a brother.

Then women began to screech from the crag above,
Gaelic keenings and cursings.

A dozen eunuchs fell beside the porch.
The boy made a dove of his two hands.

We entered a cave of wax and perfumes.
Mund took a silver cup from a niche.

Cold tinklings like nails
Took us to nothing – a crust, a red splash.

Soon that hive was all smoke and stickiness.

We brought a fair cargo down to the *Skua.*
The abbot had called that treasure "moth-food"

Sunset. Sharing of spoils. A harp-stroke.
Soon I drifted into the stone of sleep.

SEA VILLAGE

There he rides now. Look. The laird.
A brace of grouse to the Manse.
One hand on the rein long and white and scented.

Every boat in the voe his, and the gear.
He fixes the price of the catch.
But a certain fisherman has laid his own keel.

The store? That's his too. After dark
It's a shebeen, with a crock
Of peatsmoke whisky. A man can drink till he falls.

The fisherman's mother bides here, a good woman.
Every tramp, with her, is a prince.
It's her boy, Ollie Manson, that's building the boat.

The whole parish forbidden to help him.
But Simon left his threshing
And brought hammer and rivets down to the rock.

And Vera, when he humped over the tarpot
Came with a jar from the burn.
His face flashed once in the grey water.

A black lamp in a window there. Look.
But after nightfall
Moths and men flutter her flame. The slut.

The five widows of the *Hopeful*
In this one threshold,
Rock-gathered, like stormbirds, head into wind.

Socialist books, that was the start of it.
I blame the dominie.
Paine and Blatchford, they'll bring him down.

It'll end with lawmen and prison.
They'll strip his eaves.
The mother will sit under a bare rooftree.

No need to tell you, with the clang and reek,
Who's shuttered here.
The blacksmith hammering nails for the Hall.

That's it now, on the noust, the *Equality*.
"The yawl is finished!"
The yawl is finished. More than a yawl is finished.

L. Smith, Joiner. Always a coffin on hand.
Never a smile on Lowrie
But when a window goes blind in some croft.

Up there, among the cornfields, the kirk
Cold as a sunk creel.
On a Sabbath, sea voices shake the stone.

CREATOR

He is the Grain of Dust and the Raindrop.

He is Leaf and Forest and Fall.

'Where wert thou, angel, when I came to this stone?'

He is the Pitcher at the fountain.

He is the Winter Tree dragged by a peasant.

He is Flax and Wheel and Fold of linen.

'It was my hands and knees fashioned the earth;
suffering I lay upon
chaos; then galaxies
grew from my fingers'.

He is the Street where the Daughters of Music
foregather.

'I beheld again, marvelling, the atoms that
compose the worm'.

He is Adam undone by the loom.

He is Three Nails, least fruit of the Forge.

He is the Black Diamond at the centre of time,
burnt out now.

He is the Hollow in the Rock.

He is the Seed locked in the House of Dust.

KINGDOM OF DUST

This the inheritance – slaves and exhausted earth,
A botched kingdom.

Three years he went, therefore, dropping seed
In drained dunged plough-broken glebes.

For that usurpation
He was brought before the seven corrupt stewarts.

'Let him,' they said, 'be given to the heaviest millstones.'

The dust of his eye, blood-crusted
Turned from the immaculate dust that had cloistered him.

The shoulder was broken
That had fashioned from dust shoulders of ploughman and
blacksmith.

He put the red mud of his face in a crumpled mirror.

The turning earth scraped at his hands, knees, eyes.

He had fashioned from dust mouths for the daughters of
music.
'Lament well, stone wombs, now.'

The sun, turning, uttered more burning grains.

He suffered himself to become, on a hill,
Starker than seed or star.

His dust was stirred with nails, thorns, vinegar, spearthrust,
All sharpness.

He hung, the Man of Dust, a whisper
In the noonday of nothing.

They gave his dust back to that purest of urns.

Then they locked their king in a cave
Far from the turning querns of earth and sun.

CARPENTER

'Workman, what will you make on the bench today?'
I was going to hammer a crib for Mary.

I went into a multitude of green shadows, early.
I came to the marked tree at last.

I struck the root with my axe.
It groaned in the dust.

Mary came over the fields to call me to dinner –
One glance among trembling branches.

The woodman humped it into the village,
A length of gnarls and knots. A bad bargain.

Could it yield, perhaps,
A wheel for the spinning of coarse yarn?

(It looked ancient enough, that tree, to have carried the seed
Of Adam's Fall.)

I could drag out of the darkness of it, I suppose,
A board
Or wash-tub or shelf or churn, for the village women
– Never a crib for Mary's boy.

I let it lie
Among the adzes and squares, in a dazzle of sawdust, all
morning.

I lopped, later, boughs and branches and bark.

Then a centurion came
And ordered, in the governor's name, a gallows.

That's all it's good for indeed, a tree of death.

Mary stood in the door, curling cold hands like leaves
Round the fruit in her womb.

'Hurry,' she said. 'Let the saw sing.
Soon it will be time for the cradle to rock my boy.'